Hecuba by Euripides

Translated from the Greek by Theodore Alois Buckley

Euripides is rightly lauded as one of the great dramatists of all time. In his lifetime, he wrote over 90 plays and although only 18 have survived they reveal the scope and reach of his genius.

Euripides is identified with many theatrical innovations that have influenced drama all the way down to modern times, especially in the representation of traditional, mythical heroes as ordinary people in extraordinary circumstances.

As would be expected from a life lived 2,500 years ago, details of it are few and far between. Accounts of his life, written down the ages, do exist but whether much is reliable or surmised is open to debate.

Most accounts agree that he was born on Salamis Island around 480 BC, to mother Cleito and father Mnesarchus, a retailer who lived in a village near Athens. Upon the receipt of an oracle saying that his son was fated to win "crowns of victory", Mnesarchus insisted that the boy should train for a career in athletics.

However, what is clear is that athletics was not to be the way to win crowns of victory. Euripides had been lucky enough to have been born in the era as the other two masters of Greek Tragedy; Sophocles and Æschylus. It was in their footsteps that he was destined to follow.

His first play was performed some thirteen years after the first of Socrates plays and a mere three years after Æschylus had written his classic The Oristria.

Theatre was becoming a very important part of the Greek culture. The Dionysia, held annually, was the most important festival of theatre and second only to the fore-runner of the Olympic games, the Panathenia, held every four years, in appeal.

Euripides first competed in the City Dionysia, in 455 BC, one year after the death of Æschylus, and, incredibly, it was not until 441 BC that he won first prize. His final competition in Athens was in 408 BC. The Bacchae and Iphigenia in Aulis were performed after his death in 405 BC and first prize was awarded posthumously. Altogether his plays won first prize only five times.

Euripides was also a great lyric poet. In Medea, for example, he composed for his city, Athens, "the noblest of her songs of praise". His lyric skills however are not just confined to individual poems: "A play of Euripides is a musical whole....one song echoes motifs from the preceding song, while introducing new ones."

Much of his life and his whole career coincided with the struggle between Athens and Sparta for hegemony in Greece but he didn't live to see the final defeat of his city.

Euripides fell out of favour with his fellow Athenian citizens and retired to the court of Archelaus, king of Macedon, who treated him with consideration and affection.

At his death, in around 406BC, he was mourned by the king, who, refusing the request of the Athenians that his remains be carried back to the Greek city, buried him with much splendor within his own dominions. His tomb was placed at the confluence of two streams, near Arethusa in Macedonia, and a cenotaph was built to his memory on the road from Athens towards the Piraeus.

Index of Contents

INTRODUCTION

Euripides, son of Mnesarchus, was born in the island of Salamis, on the day of the celebrated victory (B.C. 480). His mother, Clito, had been sent thither in company with the other Athenian women, when Attica was given up, and the ships became at once the refuge of the male population, and the national defense. Mr. Donaldson[1] well remarks, that the patronymic form of his name, derived from the Euripus, which was the scene of the first successful resistance offered to the Persian navy, shows that the attention of his parents was fully excited by the stirring events of the time.

Notwithstanding the fact that his mother had been an herb-seller, it is probable that his father was a man of some family. That he was at least possessed of ample means, is evident from the care and expense bestowed upon our poet's education. Under the tutorship of Anaxagoras, Prodicus, and Protagoras, he had studied both natural philosophy and rhetoric in its sophistical form. In gymnastic exercises he exhibited a successful prowess, being twice victorious in the Eleusinian and Thesean games. Of his skill in painting, some specimens were preserved at Megara.

His appearance as a dramatist was at an earlier age than that of his predecessors, as he was only five and twenty years old when he produced the "Peliades," his first tragedy. On this occasion, he gained the third prize in the tragic contests, but the first, fourteen years after, and subsequently, with the "Hippolytus," in 428 B.C. The peculiar tendency of some of the ideas expressed in his plays, was the probable cause of the retirement of Euripides to Macedonia, where he obtained the friendship of King Archelaus. Perhaps, however, the unhappiness of his connubial state, arising from the infidelity of his two wives, might have rendered Athens a disagreeable place of abode for the woman-hating poet, especially when his "domestic bliss" was continually seasoned by the sarcastic jokes and allusions of his political enemy, Aristophanes. Moreover, his acquaintance with the talking philosopher, Socrates, must have been unfavorable to the continuance of his popularity.

The fate of Pentheus in our author's noble play, the "Bacchæ," appears to have given origin to the tradition that he himself was torn to pieces by dogs. If we reflect that this play was probably the last of his works, the mistake seems a plausible one. The death of Euripides, which probably happened in the ordinary course of nature, has, like that of Æschylus, been associated with the marvelous.

The Athenians vainly craved the honor of giving a resting-place to the ashes of their philosopher-poet. He was buried at Pella, but a cenotaph at Athens showed that his countrymen had not forgotten Euripides. His death took place B.C. 406.

The inferiority of our author to the greater tragedians, prevents our feeling much desire to enter upon the respective merits and demerits of his several plays, especially as we are completely anticipated by Schlegel, with whose masterly analysis every reader ought to be acquainted. Nevertheless, a few general remarks may, perhaps, be not wholly unprofitable.

It has been truly remarked, that tragedy, in no small degree, owed its downfall to Euripides. Poetry was gradually superseded by rhetoric, sublimity by earnestness, pathos by reasoning. Thus, Iphigenia and Macaria give so many good reasons for dying, that the sacrifice appears very small, and a modern wag in the upper regions of the theatre would, at the end of the speech of the latter heroine, almost have exclaimed, "Then why don't you die?"

It has been said, that our poet drew the characters of life as he found them, but bad as his characters are, they exhibit only a vulgar wickedness. Unable to portray a Clytæmnestra, he revels in the continual paltriness of a Menelaus or Ulysses. As if he took a delight in the black side of humanity, he loves to show the strength of false reasoning, of sophistry antagonistic to truth, and of cold expediency in opposition to the natural feelings of humanity. From a similar reason, his occasional attempts at comedy degenerate into mere farce. We question whether the scene between Death and Apollo in the "Alcestis," could be surpassed in vulgarity, even by the modern school of English dramatists, while his exaggerations in the minor characters are scarcely to be surpassed by the lowest writer of any period.

Under Euripides, the stage began gradually to approximate more closely to the ordinary and, at that time, debased character of Athenian society. A contempt for the Lacedæmonians, a passionate taste for the babbling and trickery of the forum, and an attempt to depreciate the social position and influence of the weaker sex, form the most unamiable features of this change. Yet we must allow, that if Euripides has reveled in the amiabilities of a Melanippe or a Phædra, in the gentle revenge of a Medea or Hecuba, he has at the same time given us an Alcestis, the only real example of genuine conjugal affection on the Greek stage.

Nor must we forget that Euripides is a greater admirer of nature, a more complete delineator of her workings, than the two greater tragedians. He has more of illustrative philosophy, more of regard to the objects of the animated creation, the system of the universe, than his greater rivals exhibit. He is, as Vitruvius has justly styled him, a "stage-philosopher." Did we possess a larger acquaintance with the works of Parmenides, Empedocles, and other early cosmogonists, we should perhaps think less of his merits on this head: as it is, the possession of some such fragments of our poet makes us deeply regret the loss of the plays themselves.

But his very love for the contemplation of nature has in no small degree contributed to the mischievous skepticism promulgated by our poet. In early times, when a rural theogony was the standard of belief, when each star had its deity, each deity its undisputed, unquestioned prerogative and worship, there was little inclination, less opportunity, for skepticism. Throughout the poetry of Hesiod, we find this feeling ever predominant, a feeling which Virgil and Tibullus well knew how to appreciate. Even Euripides himself, perhaps taught by some dangerous lessons at home, has expressed his belief that it is best "not to be too clever in matters regarding the Gods."[2] A calm retreat in the wild, picturesque tracts of Macedonia, might have had some share in reforming this spoiled pupil of the sophists. But as we find that the too careful contemplation of nature degenerates into superstition or rationalism in their various forms, so Euripides had imbibed the taste for saying startling things,[3] rather than wise; for reducing the principles of creation to materialism, the doctrines of right and wrong to expediency, and immutable truths to a popular system of question and answer. Like the generality of sophists, he took away a received truth, and left nothing to supply its place; he reasoned falsehood into probability, truth into nonentity.

At a period when the Prodico-Socratic style of disputing was in high fashion, the popularity of Euripides must have been excessive. His familiar appeals to the trifling matters of ordinary life, his characters all philosophizing, from the prince to the dry-nurse, his excellent reasons for doing right or wrong, as the case might be, must have been inestimably delightful to the accommodating morals of the Athenians. The Court of Charles the Second could hardly have derived more pleasure from the writings of a Behn or a Hamilton, than these unworthy descendants of Codrus must have experienced in hearing a bad cause so cleverly defended. Whether the orators and dikasts followed the example of the stage in those days, can scarcely be ascertained, but it is more than certain that they practically illustrated its principles. At least, the Sicilians were so fond of our author, that a few of the unfortunate survivors of the Syracusan disaster, were enabled to pick up a living by quoting such passages of our author as they had learned by heart. A compliment paid to few living dramatists in our days!

In dramatic conduct, Euripides is at an even greater disadvantage with Æschylus and Sophocles. The best characters of the piece are often the least employed, as in the instance of Macaria in the "Heraclidæ," while the play is dwindled away with dull, heavy dirges, and the complaints of senile childishness. The chorus, as Aristotle[4] has remarked, is most unfortunately independent of the plot, although the finest poetry is generally to be found in the lyric portions of our author's plays. In fact, Euripides rather wanted management in employing his resources, than the resources themselves. An ear well attuned to the harmony of verse, a delicate perception of the graceful points of language, and a finished subtilty in touching the more minute feelings and impulses of the mind, were all thrown away either upon bad subjects or worse principles. There is no true tragedy in Euripides, He is a melodramatist, but not according to the modern acceptation. His plays might end either happily or the reverse. A deity conveniently brought in, the arrival of a messenger, however unexpectedly, together with a liberal allowance for a cowardly revenge upon the vanquished—these are the Euripidean elements for giving a tragic end to a play. Nay, so great is the prodigality of slaughter throughout his dramas, that we can but imagine morbid cruelty to have formed a considerable ingredient in the disposition of Euripides. Even his pathos is somewhat tinctured with this taste for painful images. As we have beheld in our own times a barbarian alternately glut his sight with executions, and then shed floods of tears, and sink into idiot despondency; so the poetry of Euripides in turn disgusts us with outrageous cruelty, and depresses us with the most painful demands upon our compassion.

In the lyric portions of his dramas, our poet has been far more successful. The description of the capture of Troy by night,[5] is a splendid specimen of animation blended with true pathos. But taken as a whole. Euripides is a most unequal author. We may commence a play with pleasure (but O for the prologues!), we may proceed with satisfaction, but the feeling rarely lasts to the end. If I may venture an opinion upon so uncertain a subject, I should name the Hippolytus, Ion, Troades, Bacchæ, and Iphigenia in Aulis as his best plays, placing the Phœnissæ, Alcestis, Medea, Hecuba, and Orestes in a lower rank. The Helena is an amusing heap of absurdities, and reads much better in the burlesque of Aristophanes; the Electra is utterly beneath criticism; the Cyclops a weak, but humorous imitation of Homer. The other plays appear to be neither bad nor good.

The style of Euripides is, generally speaking, easy; and I can mention no author from whom a taste for elegant Greek and a facility in composition can more easily be derived. Some of his plays have suffered severely from the ravages of time, the ignorance of copyists, and the more dangerous officiousness of grammarians. Some passages of the Bacchæ, Rhesus, Troades, and the two Iphigenias, despite the ingenuity and erudition of such scholars as Porson, Elmsley, Monk, Burges, and a host of others, must still remain mere matter for guessing. Hermann's Euripides is, as a whole, sadly unworthy the abilities of the Humboldt of Greek literature.

The present volume contains the most popular of our author's works, according to present usage. But the spirit which is gradually infusing itself into the minds of those who are most actively engaged in the educational system of England, fully warrants a hope that Porson's "four plays" will shortly cease to be the boundaries of the student's acquaintance with Euripides.

I need scarcely observe, that the study of Aristophanes is indissolubly connected with that of our author. If the reader discover the painful fact that the burlesque writer is greater than the tragedian, he will perhaps also recollect that such a literary relation is, unfortunately, by no means confined to the days of Aristophanes.

Notes on the Introduction
[1] See Theatre of the Greeks, p. 92. sqq.
[2] Bacch. 200. This play was written during his sojourn with Archelaus.
[3] τοιουτονι τι παρακεκινδευμενον. Aristoph. Ran. 99.
[4] Poet. § xviii.
[5] Hec. 905 sqq.

HECUBA

THE PERSONS
GHOST OF POLYDORE.
HECUBA.
CHORUS OF FEMALE CAPTIVES.
POLYXENA.
ULYSSES.
TALTHYBIUS.
FEMALE ATTENDANT.
AGAMEMNON.
POLYMESTOR AND HIS CHILDREN.

SCENE

Before the Grecian tents, on the coast of the Thracian Chersonese.

THE ARGUMENT

After the capture of Troy, the Greeks put into the Chersonese over against Troas, But Achilles, having appeared by night, demanded one of the daughters of Priam to be slain. The Greeks therefore, in honor to their hero, tore Polyxena from Hecuba, and offered her up in sacrifice. Polymestor moreover, the king of the Thracians, murdered Polydore, a son of Priam's. Now Polymestor had received him from the hands of Priam as a charge to take care of, together with some money. But when the city was taken, wishing to seize upon his wealth, he determined to dispatch him, and disregarded the ill-fated friendship that subsisted between them; but his body being cast out into the sea, the wave threw him up on the shore before the tents of the captive women. Hecuba, on seeing the corse, recognized it; and having imparted her design to Agamemnon, sent for Polymestor to come to her with his sons, concealing what had happened, under pretense that she might discover to him some treasures hidden in Ilium. But on his arrival she slew his sons, and put out his eyes; but pleading her cause before the Greeks, she gained it over her accuser (Polymestor). For it was decided that she did not begin the cruelty, but only avenged herself on him who did begin it.

HECUBA

GHOST OF POLYDORE

GHOST OF POLYDORE
I am present, having left the secret dwellings of the dead and the gates of darkness, where Pluto has his abode apart from the other Gods, Polydore the son of Hecuba the daughter of Cisseus,[1] and Priam my sire, who when the danger of falling by the spear of Greece was threatening the city of the Phrygians, in fear, privately sent me from the Trojan land to the house of Polymestor, his Thracian friend, who cultivates the most fruitful soil of the Chersonese, ruling a warlike people with his spear.[2] But my father sends privately with me a large quantity of gold, in order that, if at any time the walls of Troy should fall, there might not be a lack of sustenance for his surviving children. But I was the youngest of the sons of Priam; on which account also he sent me privately from the land, for I was able neither to bear arms nor the spear with my youthful arm. As long then indeed as the landmarks of the country remained erect, and the towers of Troy were unshaken, and Hector my brother prevailed with his spear, I miserable increased vigorously as some young branch, by the nurture I received at the hands of the Thracian, my father's friend. But after that both Troy and the life of Hector were put an end to, and my father's mansions razed to the ground, and himself falls at the altar built by the God, slain by the blood-polluted son of Achilles, the friend of my father slays me, wretched man, for the sake of my gold, and having slain me threw me into the surf of the sea, that he might possess the gold himself in his palace. But I am exposed on the shore, at another time on the ocean's surge, borne about by many ebbings and flowings of the waves, unwept, unburied; but at present I am hastening on my dear mother's account, having left my body, borne aloft this day already the third,[3] for so long has my wretched mother been present in this territory of the Chersonese from Troy. But all the Grecians, holding their ships at anchor, are sitting quiet on the shores of this land of Thrace. For Achilles the son of Peleus, appearing above his tomb, stayed all the army of the Grecians as they were directing homeward their sea dipped oars; and asks to receive my sister Polyxena as a dear victim, and a tribute of honor to his tomb. And this he will obtain, nor will he be without this gift from his friends; and fate this day leads forth my sister to death. But my mother will see the two corses of her two children, both mine and the unhappy virgin's; for I shall appear on a breaker before the feet of a female slave, that I wretched may obtain sepulture; for I have successfully entreated those who have power beneath to find a tomb, and to fall into my mother's hands. As much then as I wish to have shall be mine; but I will withdraw myself out of the way of the aged Hecuba, for she is advancing her step beyond the tent of Agamemnon, dreading my phantom. Alas! O my mother, who, from kingly palaces, hast beheld the day of slavery, how unfortunate art thou now, in the degree that thou wert once fortunate! but some one of the Gods counterpoising your state, destroys you on account of your ancient prosperity.

HECUBA. CHORUS.

HECUBA
Lead onward, ye Trojan dames, the old woman before the tent; lead onward, raising up one now your fellow-slave, but once your queen; take me, bear me, conduct me, support my body, holding

my aged hand; and I, leaning on the bending staff of my hand,[4] will hasten to put forward the slow motion of my joints. O lightning of Jove! O thou gloomy night! why, I pray, am I thus disquieted in the night with terrors, with phantoms? O thou venerable Earth, the mother of black-winged dreams, I renounce the nightly vision, which regarding my son who is preserved in Thrace, and regarding Polyxena my dear daughter, in my dreams have I beheld, a fearful sight, I have learned, I have understood. Gods of this land, preserve my son, who, my only son, and, [as it were,] the anchor of my house, inhabits the snowy Thrace under the protection of his father's friend. Some strange event will take place, some strain will come mournful to the mournful. Never did my mind so incessantly shudder and tremble. Where, I pray, ye Trojan dames, can I behold the divine spirit of Helenus, or Cassandra, that they may interpret my dreams? For I beheld a dappled hind torn by the blood-stained fang of the wolf, forcibly dragged from my bosom, a miserable sight. And dreadful this vision also; the spectre of Achilles came above the summit of his tomb, and demanded as a tribute of honor one of the wretched Trojan women. From my daughter then, from my daughter avert this fate, ye Gods, I implore you.

CHORUS
Hecuba, with haste to thee I flew, leaving the tents of our lords, where I was allotted and ordained a slave, driven from the city of Troy, led captive of the Greeks by the point of the spear, not to alleviate aught of your sufferings, but bringing a heavy weight of tidings, and to thee, O lady, a herald of woe. For it is said that it has been decreed in the full council of the Greeks to make thy daughter a sacrifice to Achilles: for you know how that having ascended o'er his tomb, he appeared in his golden arms and restrained the fleet ships, as they were setting their sails with their halliards, exclaiming in these words; "Where speed ye, Grecians, leaving my tomb unhonored!" Then the waves of great contention clashed together, and a divided opinion went forth through the army of the Greeks; to some it appeared advisable to give a victim to his tomb, and to others it appeared not. But Agamemnon was studious to advance your good, cherishing the love of the infuriated prophetess. But the two sons of Theseus, scions of Athens, were the proposers of different arguments, but in this one opinion they coincided, to crown the tomb of Achilles with fresh blood; and declared they would never prefer the bed of Cassandra before the spear of Achilles. And the strength of the arguments urged on either side was in a manner equal, till that subtle adviser, that babbling knave,[5] honeyed in speech, pleasing to the populace, that son of Laertes, persuades the army, not to reject the suit of the noblest of all the Greeks on account of a captive victim, and not to put it in the power of any of the dead standing near Proserpine to say that the Grecians departed from the plains of Troy ungrateful to the heroes who died for the state of Greece. And Ulysses will come only not now, to tear your child from your bosom, and to take her from your aged arms. But go to the temples, speed to the altars, sit a suppliant at the knees of Agamemnon, invoke the Gods, both those of heaven, and those under the earth; for either thy prayers will prevent thy being deprived of thy wretched daughter, or thou must behold the virgin falling before the tomb, dyed in blood gushing forth in a dark stream from her neck adorned with gold.[6]

HECUBA
Alas! wretched me! what shall I exclaim? what shriek shall I utter? what lamentation? miserable through miserable age, and slavery not to be endured, insupportable. Alas! who is there to defend me? what offspring, what city! The old man is gone. My children are gone. Whither shall I turn me? and whither shall I go? Where is any god or deity to succor me? O Trojan dames, bearers of evil tidings, bearers of woe, you have destroyed me utterly, you have destroyed me. Life in the light is no more desirable! O wretched foot, lead, lead an aged woman to this tent! O child, daughter of the most afflicted mother, come forth, come forth from the tent, hear thy mother's voice, that thou mayest know what a report I hear that concerns thy life.

HECUBA, POLYXENA, CHORUS.

POLYXENA

O mother, why dost thou call! proclaiming what new affliction hast thou frighted me from the tent, as some bird from its nest, with this alarm?

HECUBA

Alas! my child!

POLYXENA

Why address me in words of ill omen? This is an evil prelude.

HECUBA

Alas! for thy life.

POLYXENA

Speak, conceal it no longer from me. I fear, I fear, my mother; why I pray dost thou groan?

HECUBA

O child, child of an unhappy mother!

POLYXENA

Why sayest thou this?

HECUBA

My child, the common decree of the Greeks unites to slay thee at the tomb of the son of Peleus.

POLYXENA

Alas, my mother! how are you relating unenviable ills? Tell me, tell me, my mother.

HECUBA

I declare, my child, the ill-omened report, they bring word that a decree has passed by the vote of the Greeks regarding thy life.

POLYXENA

O thou that hast borne affliction! O thou wretched on every side! O mother unhappy in your life, what most hated and most unutterable calamity has some destiny again sent against thee! This child is no longer thine; no longer indeed shall I miserable share slavery with miserable age. For as a mountain whelp or heifer shalt thou wretched behold me wretched torn from thine arms, and sent down beneath the darkness of the earth a victim to Pluto, where I shall lie bound in misery with the dead. But it is for thee indeed, my afflicted mother, that I lament in these mournful strains, but for my life, my wrongs, my fate, I mourn not; but death, a better lot, has befallen me.

CHORUS

But see Ulysses advances with hasty step, to declare to thee, Hecuba, some new determination.

ULYSSES, HECUBA, POLYXENA, CHORUS.

ULYSSES

Lady, I imagine that you are acquainted with the decree of the army, and the vote which has prevailed; nevertheless, I will declare it. It has been decreed by the Greeks to offer on the lofty mound of Achilles's tomb thy daughter Polyxena. But they order me to conduct and convey the damsel; but the son of Achilles is appointed to be the priest, and to preside over the rites. Do you know then what to do? Be not dragged away by violence, nor enter into a contest of strength with me, but acknowledge superior force and the presence of thy ills; it is wise to have proper sentiments even in adversity.

HECUBA
Alas! alas! the great trial is at hand, as it seems, of lamentations full, nor without tears; for I have not died in the state in which I ought to have died, nor hath Jove destroyed me, but preserves me, that I wretched may behold other misfortunes greater than [past] misfortunes. But if it be allowed slaves to put questions to the free, not offensive nor grating to the feelings, it will be your part to be questioned, and ours who are asking to attend.

ULYSSES
You have permission, ask freely, I grudge not the time.

HECUBA
Dost thou remember when thou camest a spy on Troy, disfigured by a vile dress, and from thine eyes drops caused by the fear of death bedewed thy beard?

ULYSSES
I remember well; for it made no slight impression on my heart.

HECUBA
But Helen knew thee, and told me alone.

ULYSSES
I remember the great danger I encountered.

HECUBA
And didst thou embrace my knees in thy humility?

ULYSSES
So that my hand was numbered[7] through fear on thy garments.

HECUBA
What then didst thou say, being then my slave?

ULYSSES
Many arguments that I invented to save me from death.

HECUBA
Did I preserve thee then, and conduct thee safe from the land?

ULYSSES
Yes, so that I now behold the light of the sun.

HECUBA
Art thou not then convicted of baseness by this conduct, who hast received benefits from me such as thou acknowledgest thou hast, and doest us no good in return, but evil, as far as in thee lies? Thankless is your race, as many of you as court honor from oratory before the populace; be ye not known to me, who care not to injure your friends, provided you say what is gratifying to the people.

But plotting what dark design have they determined upon a decree of death against my child? Did fate impel them to offer human sacrifices at the tomb, where it were rather right to sacrifice cattle? Or does Achilles, desirous of devoting in his turn to death those that wrought his death, with a color of justice meditate her destruction? But she has done him no ill: he should demand Helen as a sacrifice on his tomb; for she destroyed him, and brought him to Troy. But if some captive selected from the rest, and excelling in beauty, ought to die, this is not ours. For the daughter of Tyndarus is most preeminent in beauty, and has been found to be no less injurious than us. On the score of justice then I urge this argument; but with respect to what you ought to repay at my demand, hear: thou hast touched my hand, as thou ownest, and this aged cheek also, falling at my knees. Thy hand and knees I in return grasp, and re-demand the favor I granted you then, and beseech you, do not tear my child from my arms, nor kill her; enough have died already. In her I rejoice, and forget my misfortunes; she serves as my consolation in the stead of many things, she is my city, my nurse, my staff, the guide of my way. It becomes not those who have power to exercise their power in things wherein they ought not, nor should the fortunate imagine their fortune will last forever. For I too have had my time of prosperity, but now have I ceased to be: one day wrenched from me all my happiness. But by thy beard which I supplicate, reverence me, pity me; go to the Grecian army, and remind them that it is a shameful thing to slay women whom ye have once spared, and that too dragging them from the altar. But show mercy. But the laws of blood among you are laid down alike for the free and the slave. But your worth will carry with it persuasion, although your arguments be bad; for the same words from those of little character, have not the same force as when they proceed from those of high reputation.

CHORUS
There is no nature of man so obdurate, which on hearing thy groans, and thy long plaints of misery, would not let fall the tear.

ULYSSES
Hecuba, be advised, nor through passion deem him thine enemy who gives thee good advice. I indeed am ready to preserve thy person through the means of which I was fortunate; and I say no other. But what I declared before all I will not deny, that, Troy being captured, we should give thy daughter as a victim to the noblest man of the army, who demands her; for in this many cities fail, when any man who is brave and zealous receives no more honor than those who are less valiant. But Achilles, O lady, is worthy of honor from us, a man who died most gloriously in behalf of the Grecian country. Were not then this disgraceful, if when living we treat him as a friend, but after he is gone we no longer treat him so? Well! what then will any one say, if there again should be an assembling of the army, and a contest with the enemy: "Shall we fight or preserve our lives, seeing that he who falls lies unhonored?" But for me at least, living from day to day, although I have but little, that little is sufficient; but I would wish that my monument should be beheld crowned with honor, for the gratification is for a long time. But if thou sayest thou sufferest affliction, hear this in return from me. There are with us aged matrons, and hoary sires, not less wretched than thou art, and brides bereft of the noblest husbands, whose ashes this land of Troy conceals. Endure this. But we, if we injudiciously determine to honor the brave man, shall incur the charge of folly. But you barbarians neither consider your friends as friends, nor do you hold up to admiration those who have died honorably; thus shall Greece be prosperous, but you shall experience fortune corresponding to your counsels.

CHORUS
Alas! alas! how wretched is the state of slavery, and to endure indignities compelled by superior force!

HECUBA

O daughter, my words respecting thy death are vanished in the air, set forth in vain; but thou, if thou hast greater powers [of persuasion] than thy mother, use all thy influence, uttering every note as the throat of the nightingale, that thou mayest not be deprived of life. But fall before the knees of Ulysses in all the eloquence of grief, and persuade him; thou hast a pretext, for he also hath children; so that he may be inclined to pity thy fortune.

POLYXENA
I see, Ulysses, that thou art hiding thy hand beneath thy robe, and turnest thy face away, that I may not touch thy beard. Be not afraid; thou hast avoided my suppliant Jove; for I will follow thee both on account of fate, and even wishing to die; but if I were not willing, I should appear base, and too fond of life. For wherefore should I live, whose father was monarch of all the Trojans; this my dawn of life. Then was I nurtured under fair hope, a bride for princes, having no small competition for my hand, to whose palace and hearth I should come. But I, wretched now, was mistress among the Trojan women, and conspicuous in the train of virgins, equal to goddesses, death only excepted. But now I am a slave; first of all the very name, not being familiar, persuades me to love death. Then perhaps I might meet with masters cruel in disposition, who will buy me for silver, the sister both of Hector and many other [heroes.] And imposing the task of making bread in his palace, will compel me, passing the day in misery, both to sweep the house, and stand at the loom. And some slave somewhere purchased will defile my bed, before wooed by princes. This never shall be. I will quit this light from mine eyes free, offering my body to Pluto. Lead on then, Ulysses, conduct me to death; for I see neither confidence of hope, nor of expectation, present to me that I can ever enjoy good fortune. But do thou, my mother, in no wise hinder me by your words or by your actions; but assent to my death before I meet with indignities unsuited to my rank. For one who has not been accustomed to taste misfortunes bears indeed, but grieves, to put his neck under the yoke. But he would be far more blessed in death than in life; for to live otherwise than honorably is a great burden.

CHORUS
It is a great and distinguishing feature among men to be born of generous parents, and the name of nobility of birth among the illustrious, proceeds from great to greater still.

HECUBA
You have spoken honorably, my daughter, but in that honorable dwells grief. But if the son of Peleus must be gratified, and you must escape blame, Ulysses, kill not her; but leading me to the pyre of Achilles, strike me, spare me not; I brought forth Paris, who destroyed the son of Thetis, having pierced him with his arrows.

ULYSSES
The phantom of Achilles did not demand that thou, O aged lady, but that thy daughter here should die.

HECUBA
Do thou then at least slay me with my daughter, and there will be twice the libation of blood for the earth, and the dead who makes this request.

ULYSSES
Thy daughter's death suffices; one must not be heaped on another; would that we required not even this one.

HECUBA
There is a strong necessity for me to die with my daughter.

ULYSSES

How so? for I am not aware of any master that I have.

HECUBA

As the ivy the oak, so will I clasp her.

ULYSSES

Not so; if you will take the advice of your superiors in knowledge.

HECUBA

Never will I willingly quit my child here.

ULYSSES

Nor will I leave this place without the virgin.

POLYXENA

Mother, be persuaded; and thou, son of Laertes, be gentle to a parent with reason moved to anger. But thou, O wretched mother, contend not with conquerors. Dost thou wish to fall on the earth and to wound thy aged flesh dragged by violence, and to suffer the indignity of being torn by a youthful arm? which things you will suffer. Do not, I pray thee, for it is not seemly. But, my dear mother, give me thy beloved hand, and grant me to join cheek to cheek; since never hereafter, but now for the last time shall I behold the rays of the sun and his bright orb. Receive my last address, O mother! O thou that bearedst me, I am going below.

HECUBA

And I, O daughter, shall be a slave in the light of day.

POLYXENA

Without the bridegroom, without the bridal song, which I ought to have obtained.

HECUBA

Mournful thou, my child; but I am a wretched woman.

POLYXENA

There shall I lie in darkness far from thee.

HECUBA

Alas me, what shall I do? where end my life?

POLYXENA

I shall die a slave, born of a free father.

HECUBA

But I bereft indeed of fifty children.

POLYXENA

What message shall I bear to Hector, and to thy aged husband?

HECUBA

Tell them that I am most miserable of all women.

POLYXENA

O ye breasts that tenderly nursed me.

HECUBA

O daughter of an untimely and unhappy fate.

POLYXENA

Farewell, O mother, farewell Cassandra too.

HECUBA

Others farewell, but this is not for thy mother.

POLYXENA

Farewell, my brother Polydore, among the warlike Thracians.

HECUBA

If he lives at least: but I doubt, so unfortunate am I in every thing.

POLYXENA

He lives, and shall close thy dying eye.

HECUBA

I am dead, before my death, beneath my ills.

POLYXENA

Lead me, Ulysses, having covered my face with a veil, since, before I am sacrificed indeed, I am melted in heart at my mother's plaints, her also I melt by my lamentations. O light, for yet it is allowed me to express thy name, but I have no share in thee, except during the time that I am going between the sword and the pyre of Achilles.

HECUBA

Ah me! I faint; and my limbs fail me.—O daughter, touch thy mother, stretch forth thy hand—give it me—leave me not childless—I am lost, my friends. Would that I might see the Spartan Helen, the sister of the twin sons of Jove, thus, for through her bright eyes that most vile woman destroyed the happy Troy.

CHORUS

Gale, gale of the sea,[8] which waftest the swift barks bounding through the waves through the surge of the ocean, whither wilt thou bear me hapless? To whose mansion shall I come, a purchased slave? Or to the port of the Doric or Phthian shore, where they report that Apidanus, the most beautiful father of floods, enriches the plains? or wilt thou bear me hapless urged by the maritime oar, passing a life of misery in my prison-house, to that island[9] where both the first-born palm tree and the laurel shot forth their hallowed branches to their beloved Latona, emblem of the divine parturition? And with the Delian nymphs shall I celebrate in song the golden chaplet and bow of Diana? Or, in the Athenian city, shall I upon the saffron robe harness the steeds to the car of Minerva splendid in her chariot, representing them in embroidery upon the splendid looms of brilliant threads, or the race of Titans, which Jove the son of Saturn sends to eternal rest with his flaming lightning? Alas, my children! Alas, my ancestors, and my paternal land, which is overthrown, buried in smoke, captured by the Argive sword! but I indeed am[10] a slave in a foreign country, having left Asia the slave of Europe, having changed my bridal chamber for the grave.

TALTHYBIUS, HECUBA, CHORUS.

TALTHYBIUS
Tell me, ye Trojan dames, where can I find Hecuba, late the queen of Troy?

CHORUS
Not far from thee, O Talthybius, she is lying stretched on the ground, muffled in her robes.

TALTHYBIUS
O Jupiter, what shall I say? Shall I say that thou beholdest mortals? or that they have to no end or purpose entertained false notions, who suppose the existence of a race of Deities, and that fortune has the sovereign control over men? Was not this the queen of the opulent Phrygians? was not this the wife of the all-blest Priam? And now all her city is overthrown by the spear, but she a captive, aged, childless, lies on the ground defiling her ill-fated head with the dust. Alas! alas! I too am old, but rather may death be my portion before I am involved in any such debasing fortune; stand up, oh unhappy, raise thy side, and lift up thy hoary head.

HECUBA
Let me alone: who art thou that sufferest not my body to rest? why dost thou, whoever thou art, disturb me from my sadness?

TALTHYBIUS
I am here, Talthybius, the herald of the Greeks, Agamemnon having sent me for thee, O lady.

HECUBA
Hast thou come then, thou dearest of men, it having been decreed by the Greeks to slay me too upon the tomb? Thou wouldest bring dear news indeed. Then haste we, let us speed with all our might: lead on, old man.

TALTHYBIUS
I am here and come to thee, O lady, that thou mayest entomb thy dead daughter. Both the two sons of Atreus and the Grecian host send me.

HECUBA
Alas! what wilt thou say? Art thou not come for me as doomed to death, but to bring this cruel message? Thou art dead, my child, torn from thy mother; and I am childless as far as regards thee; oh! wretch that I am. But how did ye slay her? was it with becoming reverence? Or did ye proceed in your butchery as with an enemy, O old man? Tell me, though you will relate no pleasing tale.

TALTHYBIUS
Twice, O lady, thou desirest me to indulge in tears through pity for thy daughter; for both now while relating the mournful circumstance shall I bedew this eye, as did I then at the tomb when she perished. The whole host of the Grecian army was present before the tomb, at the sacrifice of thy daughter. But the son of Achilles taking Polyxena by the hand, placed her on the summit of the mound; but I stood near him: and there followed a chosen band of illustrious youths in readiness to restrain with their hands thy daughter's struggles; then the son of Achilles took a full-crowned goblet of entire gold, and poured forth libations to his deceased father; and makes signal to me to proclaim silence through all the Grecian host.

And I standing forth in the midst, thus spoke: "Be silent, O ye Greeks, let all the people remain silent; silence, be still:" and I made the people perfectly still. But he said, "O son of Peleus, O my father, accept these libations which have the power of soothing, and which speed the dead on their way; and come, that thou mayest drink the pure purple blood of this virgin, which both the army and myself offer unto thee; but be propitious to us, and grant us to weigh anchor, and to loose the cables of our ships, and to return each to his country, having met with a prosperous return from Troy." Thus much he said, and all the army joined in the prayer. Then taking by the hilt his sword decked with gold, he drew it from its scabbard, and made signs to the chosen youths of the Greeks to hold the virgin. But she, when she perceived it,[11] uttered this speech: "O Argives, ye that destroyed my city, I die willingly; let none touch my body; for I will offer my neck to the sword with a good heart. But, by the Gods, let me go free while ye kill me, that I may die free, for to be classed as a slave among the dead, when a queen, is what I am ashamed of." But the people murmured assent, and king Agamemnon ordered the young men to quit the virgin; [but they, soon as they heard the last words of him who had the seat of chief authority among them, let go their hold,] and she, on hearing this speech of her lords, took her robe, and rent it, beginning from the top of her shoulder down to her waist: and showed her breasts and bosom beauteous, as a statue's, and bending her knee on the ground, spoke words the most piteous ever heard, "Lo! strike, if this bosom thou desirest, O youth; or wouldest thou rather under the neck, here is this throat prepared." But he at once resolved and unresolved through pity of the virgin, cuts with the sword the passage of her breath; and fountains of blood burst forth. But she, e'en in death, showed much care to fall decently, and to veil from the eyes of men what ought to be concealed. But after that she breathed forth her spirit under the fatal blow, not one of the Greeks exercised the same offices; but some scattered leaves from their hands on the dead; some heap the funeral pile, bringing whole trunks of pines: but he that would not bring, heard rebukes of this sort from him that was thus employed: "Standest thou idle, thou man of most mean spirit? Hast in thy hand no robe, no ornament for the maiden? Hast thou naught to give to her so exceeding brave in heart and most noble in soul?" These things I tell thee of the death of thy daughter, but I behold thee at once the most happy, at once the most unhappy of all women in thine offspring.

CHORUS
Dreadful calamities have risen fierce against the house of Priam; such the hard fate of the Gods.

HECUBA
O daughter! which of my ills I shall first attend to, amidst such a multitude, I know not: for if I touch on any, another does not suffer me; and thence again some fresh grief draws me aside, succeeding miseries upon miseries. And now I can not obliterate from my mind thy sufferings, so as not to bewail them: but excess of grief hast thou taken away, having been reported to me as noble. Is it then no paradox, if land indeed naturally bad, when blest with a favorable season from heaven, bears well the ear; but good land, robbed of the advantages it ought to have, brings forth bad fruit: but ever among men, the bad by nature is nothing else but bad; the good always good, nor under misfortune does he degenerate from his nature, but is the same good man? Is it, that the parents cause this difference, or the education? The being brought up nobly hath indeed in it the knowledge and principles of goodness; but if one is acquainted well with this, he knows what is vicious, having already learned it by the rule of virtue. And this indeed has my mind been ejaculating in vain. But do thou go, and signify these things to the Greeks, that no one be suffered to touch my daughter, but bid them keep off the multitude. In so vast an army the rabble are riotous, and the sailors' uncontrolled insolence is fiercer than fire; and he is evil, who does not evil. But do thou, my old attendant, taking an urn, fill it with sea water, and bring it hither, that I may wash my girl in her last bath, the bride no bride now, and the virgin no longer a virgin, wash her, and lay her out; according to her merits—whence can I?

This I can not; but as I can, I will, for what can I do! And collecting ornaments from among the captured women, who dwell beside me in these tents, if any one, unobserved by our new lords, has by her any stolen memorial of her home. O state of my house, O mansions once happy! O Priam, of vast wealth possessed, and supremely blest in thine offspring, and I too, this aged woman, the mother of such children! How have we come to nothing, bereft of our former grandeur! And yet still forsooth we are elated, one of us in his gorgeous palaces; another, when honored among his citizens. These are nothing. In vain the counsels of the mind, and the tongue's boast. He is most blest, to whom from day to day no evil happens.

CHORUS

Against me was it fated that calamity, against me was it fated that woe should spring, when Paris first hewed the pine in Ida's forest, preparing to cut his way over the ocean surge to the bed of Helen, the fairest that the sun's golden beams shine upon. For toils, and fate more stern than toils, close us round: and from the folly of one came a public calamity fatal to the land of Simois, and woes springing from other woes: and when the dispute was decided, which the shepherd decided between the three daughters of the blessed Gods on Ida's top, for war, and slaughter, and the desolation of my palaces. And many a Spartan virgin at her home on the banks of the fair-flowing Eurotas sighs while bathed in tears: and many an aged matron strikes her hand against her hoary head, for her children who have perished, and tears her cheek making her nails all blood-stained with her wounds.

FEMALE ATTENDANT, CHORUS, HECUBA.

FEMALE ATTENDANT

O attendants, where, I pray, is the all-wretched Hecuba, who surpasses the whole race of man and woman kind in calamities? no one shall wrest from her the crown.

CHORUS

But what dost thou want, O wretch, in thy words of ill omen? for thy messages of woe never rest.

FEMALE ATTENDANT

I bring this grief to Hecuba; but in calamity 'tis no easy thing for men to speak words of good import.

CHORUS

And see, she is coming out of the house, and appears in the right time for thy words.

FEMALE ATTENDANT

O all-wretched mistress, and yet still more wretched than I can express in words, thou art undone, and no longer beholdest the light, childless, husbandless, cityless, entirely destroyed.

HECUBA

Thou has said nothing new, but hast reproached me who already know it: but why dost thou bring this corse of my Polyxena, whose sepulture was reported to me as in a state of active progress through the labors of all the Grecians?

FEMALE ATTENDANT

She nothing knows, but, woe's me! laments Polyxena, nor does she apprehend her new misfortunes.

HECUBA

O wretched me! dost bring hither the body of the frantic and inspired Cassandra?

FEMALE ATTENDANT

She whom thou mentionedst, lives; but thou dost not weep for him who is dead; but behold this corse cast naked [on the shore,] and look if it will appear to thee a wonder, and what thou little expectest.

HECUBA

Alas me! I do indeed see my son Polydore a corse, whom (I fondly hoped) the man of Thrace was preserving in his palace. Now am I lost indeed, I no longer exist. Oh my child, my child! Alas! I begin the Bacchic strain, having lately learned my woes from my evil genius.

FEMALE ATTENDANT

Thou knowest then the calamity of thy son, O most unfortunate.

HECUBA

I see incredible evils, still fresh, still fresh: and my immeasurable woes follow one upon the other. No longer will a day without a tear, without a groan, have part with me.

CHORUS

Dreadful, oh! dreadful are the miseries that we endure!

HECUBA

O child, child of a wretched mother, by what fate art thou dead, by what hap liest thou here? by the hand of what man?

FEMALE ATTENDANT

I know not: on the wave-washed shore I found him.

HECUBA

Cast up from the sea, or fallen by the blood-stained spear?

FEMALE ATTENDANT

The ocean's billow cast him up from the deep on the smooth sand.

HECUBA

Woe is me! Now understand I the dream, the vision of mine eyes; the black-winged phantom has not flitted by me in vain, which I saw concerning thee, my child, as being no longer in the light of day.

CHORUS

But who slew him? canst thou, O skilled in dreams, declare him?

HECUBA

My friend, my friend, who curbs the steed in Thrace, where his aged father placed him for concealment.

CHORUS

Ah me! what wilt thou say? Was it to possess his gold that he slew him!

HECUBA

Unutterable deeds, unworthy of a name, surpassing miracles, unhallowed, insufferable! Where are the laws of hospitality? O most accurst of men, how didst thou mar that skin, how sever with the cruel sword the poor limbs of this boy, nor didst feel pity?

CHORUS
O hapless woman, how has the deity made thee by far the most wretched of mortals, whoever he be that presses heavy on thee! But, my friends, let us henceforward be silent, for I see our lord Agamemnon advancing.

AGAMEMNON, CHORUS, HECUBA.

AGAMEMNON
Why, Hecuba, delayest thou to come, and bury thy girl in her tomb, agreeably to what Talthybius told me, that no one of the Argives should be suffered to touch thy daughter. For our part we leave her alone, and touch her not; but thou art slow, whereat I am astonished. I am come therefore to fetch thee, for every thing there has been well and duly performed, if aught of well there be in this. Ah! what corse is this I see before the tent? some Trojan's too? for that it is no Grecian's, the robes that vest his limbs inform me.

HECUBA (aside)
Thou ill-starr'd wretch! myself I mean, when I say "thou." O Hecuba, what shall I do? Shall I fall at the knees of Agamemnon here, or bear my ills in silence?

AGAMEMNON
Why dost lament turning thy back upon me, and sayest not what has happened? Who is this?

HECUBA (aside)
But should he, thinking me a slave, an enemy, spurn me from his knees, I should be adding to my present sufferings.

AGAMEMNON
No prophet I, so as to trace, unless by hearing, the path of thy counsels.

HECUBA (aside)
Am I not rather then putting an evil construction on this man's thoughts, whereas he has no evil intention toward me?

AGAMEMNON
If thou art willing that I should nothing of this affair, thou art of a mind with me, for neither do I wish to hear.

HECUBA (aside)
I can not without him take vengeance for my children. Why do I thus hesitate? I must be bold, whether I succeed, or fail. Agamemnon, by these knees, and by thy beard I implore thee, and by thy blessed hand—

AGAMEMNON
What thy request? Is it to pass thy life in freedom? for this is easy for thee to obtain.

HECUBA
Not this indeed; but so that I avenge myself on the bad, I am willing to pass my whole life in slavery.

AGAMEMNON
And for what assistance dost thou call on me?

HECUBA

In none of those things which thou imaginest, O king. Seest thou this corse, o'er which I drop the tear?

AGAMEMNON

I see it; thy meaning however I can not learn from this.

HECUBA

Him did I once bring forth, him bore I in my bosom.

AGAMEMNON

Is this indeed one of thy children, O unhappy woman?

HECUBA

It is, but not of the sons of Priam who fell under the walls of Troy.

AGAMEMNON

Didst thou then bear any other besides those, O lady?

HECUBA

In vain, as it appears, this whom you see.

AGAMEMNON

But where did he chance to be, when the city fell?

HECUBA

His father sent him out of the country, dreading his death.

AGAMEMNON

Whither, having removed him alone of his children then alive?

HECUBA

To this country, where he was found a corse.

AGAMEMNON

To him who is king over this state, to Polymestor?

HECUBA

Hither was he sent, the guardian of gold, which proved most destructive to him.

AGAMEMNON

By whose hand then he is dead, and having met with what fate?

HECUBA

By whom else should he? The Thracian host slew him.

AGAMEMNON

O wretch! was he so inflamed with the desire of obtaining the gold?

HECUBA

Even so, after he had heard of Troy's disasters.

AGAMEMNON
And where didst thou find him, or who brought the body?

HECUBA
She, meeting with it on the sea-shore.

AGAMEMNON
In quest of it, or occupied in some other employment?

HECUBA
She was going to bring from the sea wherewith to bathe Polyxena.

AGAMEMNON
This friend then, as it seems, murdered him, and after that cast him out.

HECUBA
To toss upon the waves thus gashing his body.

AGAMEMNON
O thou unhappy from thy unmeasured ills!

HECUBA
I perish, no woe is left, O Agamemnon.

AGAMEMNON
Alas! alas! What woman was ever so unfortunate?

HECUBA
There is none, except you reckon Misfortune herself. But for what cause I fall at thy knees, now hear: if I appear to you to suffer these ills justly, I would be reconciled to them; but if otherwise, be thou my avenger on this man, this most impious of false friends; who revering neither the Gods beneath[12] the earth, nor the Gods above, hath done this most unholy deed, having often partaken of the same table with me, [and in the list of hospitality the first of my friends; and having met with whatever was due,[13] and having received a full consideration for his services,[14]] slew him, and deigned not to give him a tomb, which he might have given, although he purposed to slay him, but cast him forth at the mercy of the waves. We indeed are slaves, and perhaps weak; but the Gods are strong, and strong the law, which governs them; for by the law we judge that there are Gods, and we live having justice and injustice strictly defined; which if when referred to thee it be disregarded, and they shall suffer no punishment who slay their guests, or dare to pollute the hallowed statutes of the Gods, there is nothing equitable in the dealings of men. Beholding these things then in a base and proper light, reverence me; pity me, and, as the artist stands aside to view a picture, do thou view my living portrait, and see what woes I am enduring. Once was I a queen, but now I am thy slave; once was I blest in my children, but now aged, and at the same time childless, cityless, destitute, the most miserable of mortals. Alas me wretched! whither withdrawest from me thy foot? It seems[15] I shall make no impression, wretch that I am. Why then do we mortals toil after all other sciences, as a matter of duty, and dive into them, but least of all strive to learn thoroughly Persuasion, the sole mistress o'er the minds of men, giving a price for her knowledge, that at some time we may have it in our power at once to persuade and obtain what we wish?—How then can any one hereafter hope that he shall be fortunate? So many children that I had, and now not one is

left to me. But I am perishing a captive in base servitude, and yet see the smoke there leaping aloft from the city. And however this part of my argument may perchance be vain, the bringing forward love; still nevertheless it shall be urged. My daughter is wont to sleep by thy side, that prophetess, whom the Trojans call Cassandra. Where wilt thou show that thy nights were nights of love, O king, or will my daughter receive any recompense for her most fond embraces, and I through her? [For from the secret shade, and from night's joys, the greatest delight is wont to spring to mortals.] Now then attend. Thou seest this corse? Him assisting, thou wilt assist one joined to thee in affinity. One thing my speech wants yet. I would fain I had a voice in my arms, and hands, and in my hair, and in my footsteps, or by the skill of Dædalus, or some God, that each at once might hold thy knees, weeping, and imploring in all the strains of eloquence. O my lord. O greatest light of the Greeks, be persuaded; lend thy hand to avenge this aged woman, although she is of no consequence, yet avenge her. For it belongs to a good man to minister justice, and always and in every case to punish the bad.

CHORUS
It is strange, how every thing happens to mortals, and laws determine even the fates, making the greatest enemies friends, and enemies of those who before were on good terms.

AGAMEMNON
I, O Hecuba, have pity both on thee and thy son, thy misfortunes, and thy suppliant touch, and I am willing in regard both to the Gods and to justice, that this impious host should give thee full revenge, provided a way could be found, that both you might be gratified, and I might in the eyes of the army not seem to meditate this destruction against the king of Thrace for Cassandra's sake. For there is a point in which apprehension hath reached me. This man the army deems a friend, the dead an enemy; but if he is dear to thee, this is a private feeling and does not affect the army. Wherefore consider, that thou hast me willing to labor with thee, and ready to assist thee, but backward, should I be murmured against among the Greeks.

HECUBA
Alas! no mortal is there who is free. For either he is the slave of money or of fortune; or the populace of the city or the dictates of the law constrain him to adopt manners not accordant with his natural inclinations. But since thou fearest, and payest too much regard to the multitude, I will liberate thee from this fear. For consent with me, if I meditate vengeance against the murderer of this youth, but do not act with me. But should any tumult or offer of assistance arise from out of the Greeks, when the Thracian feels the punishment he shall feel, suppress it, not appearing to do it for my sake: but of the rest be confident: I will dispose all things well.

AGAMEMNON
How then? What wilt thou do? Wilt thou grasp the sword in thine aged hand, and strike the barbarian? or with poison wilt thou work, or with what assistance? What hand will conspire with thee? whence wilt thou procure friends?

HECUBA
These tents inclose a host of Trojan dames.

AGAMEMNON
Meanest thou the captives, the booty of the Greeks?

HECUBA
With these will I avenge me of my murderer.

AGAMEMNON

And how shall the victory over men be to women?

HECUBA

Numbers are powerful, with stratagem invincible.

AGAMEMNON

Powerful, I grant; I mistrust however the race of women.

HECUBA

And why? Did not women slay the sons of Ægyptus,[16] and utterly extirpated the race of men from Lemnos?[17] But thus let it be. Give up this discussion. But grant this woman to pass in safety through the army. And do thou go to the Thracian host and tell him, "Hecuba, once queen of Troy, sends for you on business of no less importance to yourself than to her, and your sons likewise, since it is of consequence that your children also should hear her words."—And do thou, O Agamemnon, as yet forbear to raise the tomb over the newly-sacrificed Polyxena, that these two, the brother and the sister, the divided care of their mother, may, when reduced to ashes by one and the same flame, be interred side by side.

AGAMEMNON

Thus shall it be. And yet, if the army could sail, I should not have it in my power to grant thy request: but now, for the deity breathes not prosperous gales, we must wait, watching for a calm voyage. But may things turn out well some way or other: for this is a general principle among all, both individuals in private and states, That the wicked man should feel vengeance, but the good man enjoy prosperity.

CHORUS

O thou, my country of Troy, no longer shall thou be called the city of the invincible, such a cloud of Grecians envelops thee, with the spear, with the spear having destroyed thee. And thou hast been shorn of thy crown of turrets, and thou hast been discolored by the dismal blackness of smoke; hapless city, no longer shall I tread my steps in thee.

In the midnight hour I perished, when after the feast sweet sleep is scattered over the eyes. And my husband, from the song and cheerful sacrifice retired, was sleeping peacefully in my bed, his spear on its peg, no more dreaming to behold the naval host of the Greeks treading the streets of Troy. But I was binding my braided hair with fillets fastened on the top of mine head, looking into the round polished surface of the golden mirror, that I might get into my bed prepared for me. On a sudden a tumultuous cry penetrated the city; and this shout of exhortation was heard in the streets of Troy, "When indeed, ye sons of Grecians, when, if not now, will ye return to your homes having overthrown the proud citadel of Ilium!" And having left my dear bed, in a single robe, like a Spartan virgin, flying for aid to the venerable shrine of Diana, I hapless fled in vain. And I am dragged, after having seen my husband slain, to the ocean waves; and casting a distant look back upon my city, after the vessel had begun her way in her return to Greece, and divided me from the land of Troy, I wretched fainted through anguish. And consigning to curses Helen, the sister of the Twin Brothers, and the Idean shepherd, the ruthless Paris, since his marriage, no marriage, but some Fury's hate hath utterly destroyed me far from my native land, and hath driven me from my home. Whom may the ocean refuse ever to bear back again; and may she never reach again her paternal home.

POLYMESTOR, HECUBA, CHORUS.

POLYMESTOR

O Priam, thou dearest of men, and thou most dear Hecuba, at thy sight I weep for thee, and thy city, and thy daughter who has lately died. Alas! there is nothing secure, neither glory, nor when one is faring well is there a certainty that he will not fare ill. But the Gods mingle these things promiscuously to and fro, making all confusion, so that we through ignorance may worship them. But wherefore should I utter these plaints, which in no way tend to free thee from thy former calamities. But thou, if thou hast aught to blame for my absence, forbear; for I chanced to be afar off in the middle of my Thracian territories, when thou camest hither; but soon as I returned, as I was already setting out from my house, this maid of thine met me for the self-same purpose, and delivered thy message, which when I had heard, I came.

HECUBA

O Polymestor, I am ashamed to look thee in the face, sunk as I am in such miseries; for before one who has seen me in prosperity, shame overwhelms me, being in the state in which I now am, nor can I look upon thee with unmoved eyes. But impute not this to any enmity I bear thee; but there are other causes, and in some degree this law; "that women ought not to gaze at men."

POLYMESTOR

And 'tis indeed no wonder; but what need hast thou of me? for what purpose didst thou send for me to come from home?

HECUBA

I am desirous of communicating a private affair of my own to thee and thy children; but order thy attendants to retire from these tents.

POLYMESTOR

Depart, for here to be alone is safe. Friendly thou art, this Grecian army too is friendly toward me, but it is for thee to signify, in what manner I, who am in good circumstances, ought to succor my friends in distress; since, on my part, I am ready.

HECUBA

First then tell me of my son Polydore, whom thou retainest, receiving him from mine, and from his father's hand, if he live; but the rest I shall inquire of thee afterward.

POLYMESTOR

He lives, and in good health; as far as regards him indeed thou art happy.

HECUBA

O my best friend, how well thou speakest, and how worthily of thyself!

POLYMESTOR

What dost thou wish then to inquire of me in the next place?

HECUBA

Whether he remembers at all me, his mother?

POLYMESTOR

Yes: and he even sought to come to thee by stealth.

HECUBA

And is the gold safe, which he brought with him from Troy?

POLYMESTOR

It is safe, at least it is guarded in my house.

HECUBA

Preserve it therefore, nor covet the goods of others.

POLYMESTOR

Certainly not. May I enjoy what is mine own, O lady.

HECUBA

Knowest thou then, what I wish to say to thee and thy children?

POLYMESTOR

I do not: this shalt thou signify by thy speech.

HECUBA

Be my son loved by thee, as thou art now loved of me.

POLYMESTOR

What is it, that I and my sons must know?

HECUBA

The ancient buried treasures of the family of Priam.

POLYMESTOR

Is it this thou wishest me to inform thy son of?

HECUBA

Yes, certainly; through thee at least, for thou art a pious man.

POLYMESTOR

What necessity then is there for the presence of these children?

HECUBA

'Tis better in case of thy death, that these should know.

POLYMESTOR

Well hast thou thus said, and 'tis the wiser plan.

HECUBA

Thou knowest then where the temple of Minerva in Troy is—

POLYMESTOR

Is the gold there! but what is the mark?

HECUBA

A black rock rising above the earth.

POLYMESTOR

Hast any thing further to tell me of what is there?

HECUBA

No, but I wish thee to take care of some treasures, with which I came out of the city.

POLYMESTOR

Where are they then? Hast thou them hidden beneath thy robes?

HECUBA

Amidst a heap of spoils they are preserved in this tent.

POLYMESTOR

But where? These are the naval encampments of the Grecians.

HECUBA

The habitations of the captive women are private.

POLYMESTOR

And is all secure within, and untenanted by men?

HECUBA

Not one of the Greeks is within, but we women only. But come into the tent, for the Greeks are desirous of loosing the sheets of their vessels homeward from Troy; so that, having done every thing that thou oughtest, thou mayest go with thy children to that place where thou hast given my son to dwell.

CHORUS

Not yet hast thou suffered, but peradventure thou wilt suffer vengeance; as a man falling headlong into the gulf where no harbor is, shalt thou be hurled from thy dear heart, having lost thy life;[18] for where the rites of hospitality coincide[19] with justice, and with the Gods, on the villain who dares to violate these destructive, destructive indeed impends the evil. But thy hopes will deceive thee, which thou entertainedst from this journey, which has brought thee, thou wretched man, to the deadly mansions of Pluto; but thou shalt quit thy life by no warrior's hand.

POLYMESTOR, HECUBA, SEMI-CHORUS.

POLYMESTOR

Oh me! I wretch am deprived of the sight of mine eyes.

SEMI-CHORUS

Heard ye the shriek of the man of Thrace, my friends?

POLYMESTOR

Oh me; there again—Oh my children, thy miserable butchery!

SEMI-CHORUS

My friends, some strange ills have been perpetrated within the tents.

POLYMESTOR

But for all your nimble feet, ye never can escape me, for by my blows will I burst open the recesses of these tents.

SEMI-CHORUS

Behold, he uses violently the weapon of his heavy hand. Will ye that we fall on; since the instant calls on us to be present with assistance to Hecuba and the Trojan dames?

HECUBA

Dash on, spare nothing, break down the gates, for thou never shalt replace the clear sight in those pupils, nor shalt thou behold alive those children which I have slain.

SEMI-CHORUS

What! hast thou vanquished the Thracian? and hast thou got the mastery over this host, my mistress? and hast thou done such deeds, as thou sayest?

HECUBA

Thou wilt see him quickly before the house, blind, with blind wandering steps approaching, and the bodies of his two children, whom I have slain with these most valiant Trojan women; but he has felt my vengeance; but he is coming as thou seest from the tent. But I will retire out of his way, and make good my retreat from the boiling rage of this most desperate Thracian.

POLYMESTOR

Alas me! whither can I go? where stand? whither shall I direct my way, advancing my steps like the four-footed mountain beast on my hands and on my feet in pursuit? What new path shall I take in this direction or in that, desirous of seizing these murderous Trojan dames, who have utterly destroyed me; O ye impious, impious Phrygian daughters! Ah the accursed, in what corner do they shrink from me in flight? Would that thou, O sun, could'st heal, could'st heal these bleeding lids of my eyes, and remove this gloomy-darkness. Ah, hush, hush! I hear the carefully-concealed step of these women. Whither shall I direct my course in order that I may glut myself on the flesh and bones of these, making the wild beasts' banquet, inflicting vengeance on them, in return for the injuries done me. Wretch that I am! Whither, whither am I borne, having left my children deserted, for these fiends of hell to tear piecemeal, a mangled, bleeding, savage prey to dogs, and a thing to cast out on the mountains? Where shall I stand? Whither turn? Whither go, as a ship setting her yellow canvas sails with her sea-washed palsers, rushing to this lair of death, the protector of my children?

CHORUS

O miserable man, what intolerable evils have been perpetrated by thee! but on thee having done base deeds the God hath sent dreadful punishment, whoever he be that presses heavy on thee.

POLYMESTOR

Alas! alas! O Thracian nation, brandishing the spear, warlike, bestriding the steed, nation ruled by Mars; O ye Greeks, sons of Atreus; I raise the cry, the cry, the cry; Come, come, hasten, I entreat you by the Gods. Does any hear, or will no one assist me? Why do ye delay? The women have destroyed me, the captive women. Horrible, horrible treatment have I suffered. Alas me for my ruin! Whither can I turn? Whither can I go? Shall I soar through the ethereal skies to the lofty mansions where Orion or Sirius dart from their eyes the flaming rays of fire: or shall I hapless rush to the gloomy shore of Pluto?

CHORUS

It is pardonable, when any one suffers greater misfortunes than he can bear, for him to be desirous to quit a miserable life.

AGAMEMNON, POLYMESTOR, HECUBA, CHORUS.

AGAMEMNON

I came having heard the clamor: for Echo, the mountain's daughter, did not sound in gentle strains through the army, causing a disturbance. But did we not know that the Phrygian towers are fallen beneath the Grecian spear, this tumult might have caused no little terror.

POLYMESTOR

O my dearest friend (for I know thee, Agamemnon, having heard thy voice), seest thou what I am suffering?

AGAMEMNON

Ah! wretched Polymestor, who hath destroyed thee? who made thine eyes sightless, having drowned their orbs in blood? And who hath slain these thy children? Sure, whoe'er it was, felt the greatest rage against thee and thy sons.

POLYMESTOR

Hecuba with the female captives hath destroyed me—nay, not destroyed me, but more than destroyed me.

AGAMEMNON

What sayest thou? Hast thou done this deed, as he affirms? Hast thou, Hecuba, dared this inconceivable act of boldness?

POLYMESTOR

Ah me! what wilt thou say? Is she any where near me? Show me, tell me where she is, that I may seize her in my hands, and tear piecemeal and mangle her body.

AGAMEMNON

What ho! what are you doing?

POLYMESTOR

By the Gods I entreat thee, suffer me to lay my raging hand upon her.

AGAMEMNON

Forbear. And having banished this barbarous deed from thy thoughts, speak; that having heard both thee and her in your respective turns, I may decide justly, in return for what thou art suffering these ills.

POLYMESTOR

I will speak then. There was a certain youth, the youngest of Priam's children, by name Polydore, the son of Hecuba; him his father Priam sent to me from Troy to bring up in my palace, already presaging[20] the capture of Troy. Him I put to death. But for what cause I put him to death, with what policy and prudent forethought, now hear. I feared, lest the boy being left an enemy to thee, should collect the scattered remnants of Troy, and again people the city. And lest the Greeks, having discovered that one of the sons of Priam was alive, should again direct an expedition against the Phrygian land, and after that should harass and lay waste the plains of Thrace; and it might fare ill with the neighbors of the Trojans, under which misfortune, O king, we are now laboring. But Hecuba, when she had discovered her son's death, by such treachery as this lured me hither, as about to tell me of treasure belonging to Priam's family concealed in Troy, and introduces me alone with my sons into the tent, that no one else might know it. And I sat, having reclined on the centre of the couch; but many Trojan damsels, some from the left hand, and others from the right, sat round me, as by an intimate friend, holding in their hands the Edonian looms, and praised these robes, looking at them in the light; but others, beholding with admiration my Thracian spear, deprived me of my double ornament. But as many as were mothers caressed my children in their arms in seeming admiration, that they might be farther removed from their father, successively handing them from one to another: and then, amidst their kind blandishments, what think you? in an instant, snatching from somewhere beneath their garments their daggers, they stab my children. But they having seized me in an hostile manner held my hands and feet; and if, wishing to succor my children, I raised my head, they held me by the hair: but if I attempted to move my hands, I wretched could effect nothing through the host of women. But at last, cruelty and worse than cruelty, they perpetrated dreadful things; for having taken their clasps they pierce and gore the wretched pupils of my eyes, then vanish in flight through the tent. But I, having leaped out, like some exasperated beast, pursue the blood-stained wretches, searching every wall, as the hunter, casting down, rending. This have I suffered, while studious to advance thy interest, Agamemnon, and having killed thine enemy. But that I may not extend my speech to a greater length, if any one of those of ancient times hath reviled women, or if any one doth now, or shall hereafter revile them, I will comprise the whole when I say, that such a race neither doth the sea nor the earth produce, but he who is always with them knows it best.

CHORUS

Be not at all insolent, nor, in thy calamities, thus comprehending the female sex, abuse them all. For of us there are many, some indeed are envied for their virtues, but some are by nature in the catalogue of bad things.

HECUBA

Agamemnon, it never were fitting among men that the tongue should have greater force than actions. But if a man has acted well, well should he speak; if on the other hand basely, his words likewise should be unsound, and never ought he to be capable of speaking unjust things well. Perhaps indeed they who have brought these things to a pitch of accuracy are accounted wise, but they can not endure wise unto the end, but perish vilely, nor has any one yet escaped this. And this in my prelude is what I have to say to thee. Now am I going to direct my discourse to this man, and I will answer his arguments. Thou, that assertest, that in order to rid the Greeks of their redoubled toil, and for Agamemnon's sake that thou didst slay my son? But, in the first place, monstrous villain, never can the race of barbarians be friendly to the Grecians, never can this take place. But what favor wert thou so eagerly currying? wert thou about to contract an alliance, or was it that thou wert of kindred birth, or what pretext hadst thou? or were they about to ravage the crops of thy country, having sailed thither again? Whom, thinkest thou, wilt thou persuade of these things? The gold, if thou wert willing to speak truth, the gold destroyed my son, and thy base gains. For come, tell me this; how when Troy was prosperous, and a tower yet girt around the city, and Priam lived, and the spear of Hector was in its glory, why didst thou not then, if thou wert willing to lay him under this obligation, bringing up my child, and retaining him in thy palace, why didst thou not then slay him, or go and take him alive to the Greeks? But when we were no longer in the light of prosperity, and the city by its smoke showed that it was in the power of the enemy, thou slewest thy guest who had come to thy hearth. Now hear besides how thou wilt appear vile: thou oughtest, if thou wert the friend of the Greeks, to have given the gold, which thou confessedst thou hast, not thine, but his, distributing to those who were in need, and had long been strangers to their native land. But thou, even now, hast not courage to part with it from thy hand, but having it, thou still art keeping it close in thine house. And yet, in bringing up my child, as it was thy duty to bring him up, and in preserving him, thou hadst had fair honor. For in adversity friends are most clearly proved good. But good circumstances have in every case their friends. But if thou wert in want of money, and he in a flourishing condition, my son had been to thee a vast treasure; but now, thou neither hast him for thy friend, and the benefit from the gold is gone, and thy sons are gone, and thou art—as thou art. But to thee, Agamemnon, I say; if thou aidest this man, thou wilt appear to be doing wrong. For thou wilt be conferring a benefit on a host, who is neither pious, nor faithful to those to whom he ought, not holy, not just. But we shall say that thou delightest in the bad, if thus thou actest: but I speak no offense to my lords.

CHORUS
Ah! Ah! How do good deeds ever supply to men the source of good words!

AGAMEMNON
Thankless my office to decide on others' grievances; but still I must, for it brings disgrace on a man, having taken a thing in hand, to give it up. But to me, be assured, thou neither appearest for my sake, nor for the sake of the Grecians, to have killed this man thy guest, but that thou mightest possess the gold in thy palace. But thou talkest of thy advantage, when thou art in calamities.[21] Perhaps with you it is a slight thing to kill your guests; but with us Grecians this thing is abhorred. How then, in giving my decision that thou hast not injured, can I escape blame? I can not; but as thou hast dared to do things dishonorable, endure now things unpleasant.

POLYMESTOR
Alas me! worsted, as it seems, by a woman who is a slave, I shall submit to the vengeance of my inferiors.

AGAMEMNON
Will it not then be justly, seeing thou hast acted wrong?

POLYMESTOR
Alas me! wretched on account of these children and on account of my eyes.

HECUBA
Thou sufferest? but what do I? Thinkest thou I suffer not for my child?

POLYMESTOR
Thou rejoicest in insulting me, O thou malicious woman.

HECUBA
For ought not I to rejoice on having avenged myself on thee?

POLYMESTOR
But thou wilt not soon, when the liquid wave—

HECUBA
Shall bear me, dost thou mean, to the confines of the Grecian land?

POLYMESTOR
—shall cover thee, having fallen from the shrouds.

HECUBA
From whom meeting with this violent leap?

POLYMESTOR
Thyself shalt climb with thy feet up the ship's mast.

HECUBA

Having wings on my back, or in what way?

POLYMESTOR
Thou shalt become a dog with a fiery aspect.

HECUBA
But how dost thou know of this my metamorphose?

POLYMESTOR
Dionysius the Thracian prophet told it me.

HECUBA
But did he not declare to thee any of the evils which thou sufferest?

POLYMESTOR
No: for, if he had, thou never wouldst thus treacherously have taken me.

HECUBA
Thence shall I conclude my life in death, or still live on? [22]

POLYMESTOR
Thou shalt die. But the name of thy tomb shall be—

HECUBA
Dost thou speak of it as in any way correspondent to my shape?

POLYMESTOR
The tomb of the wretched dog, a mark to mariners. [23]

HECUBA
I heed it not, since thou at least hast felt my vengeance.

POLYMESTOR
And it is fated too for thy daughter Cassandra to die.

HECUBA
I renounce these prophecies; I give them for thyself to bear.

POLYMESTOR
Him shall his wife slay, a cruel guardian of his house.

HECUBA
Never yet may the daughter of Tyndarus have arrived at such madness.

POLYMESTOR
Even this man himself, having lifted up the axe.

AGAMEMNON
What ho! thou art mad, and art desirous of obtaining greater ills.

POLYMESTOR

Kill me, for the murderous bath at Argos awaits thee.

AGAMEMNON
Will ye not, slaves, forcibly drag him from my presence?

POLYMESTOR
Thou art galled at what thou hearest.

AGAMEMNON
Will ye not stop his mouth?

POLYMESTOR
Stop it: for the word is spoken.

AGAMEMNON
Will ye not as quick as possible cast him out on some desert island, since he is thus, and past endurance insolent? But do thou, wretched Hecuba, go and bury thy two dead: and you, O Trojan dames, must approach your masters' tents, for I perceive that the gales are favorable for wafting us to our homes. And may we sail in safety to our native country, and behold our household and families in prosperity, having found rest from these toils.

CHORUS
Come, my friends, to the harbor, and the tents, to undergo the tasks imposed by our masters. For necessity is relentless.

NOTES ON HECUBA

[1] Homer makes Dymas, not Cisseus, the father of Hecuba. Virgil however follows Euripides, the rest of the Latin poets Virgil.

[2] In the martial time of antiquity the spear was reverenced as something divine, and signified the chief command in arms, it was also the insigne of the highest civil authority: in this sense Euripides in other places uses the word δορυ. See Hippol. 988.

[3] τριταιος properly signifies triduanus; here it is used for τριτος, the cardinal number for the ordinal. So also Hippol. 275.

Πως δ' ου, τριταιαν γ' ουσ' ασιτος 'ημεραν:

[4] Most interpreters render this, leaning on the crooked staff with my hand. Nor has Beck altered it in his Latin version, though he transcribed Musgrave's note. "σκολιω, σκιμπωνι (for which Porson directs σκιπωνι,) Scipiones in universum recti sunt, non curvi. Loquitur igitur non de vero scipione, sed metaphorice de brachio, quod ancillis innitens, scipionis usum præstabat; quodque, ob cubiti flexuram, σκολιον σκιμπωμα vocat."

[5] that babbling knave.] Tzetzes on Lycophron, line 763. κοπις, 'ο 'ρητωρ, και εμπειρος, 'ο 'υπο πολλων πραγματων κεκομμενος. In the Index to Lycophron κοπις is translated scurra.

[6] Among the ancients it was the custom for virgins to have a great quantity of golden ornaments about them, to which Homer alludes, Il. B. 872.

Ὃς και χρυσον εχων πολεμον δ' ιεν ηϋτε κουρη. PORSON.

[7] This is the only sense that can be made of ενθανειν, and this sense seems strained: Brunck proposes εντακηναι for ενθανειν γε. See Note [A].

[8] λιμνη is used for the sea in Troades 444; as also in Iliad N. 21, and Odyssey Γ. 1. and in many other passages of Homer.

[9] The construction is η πορευσεις με ενθα νασων; for εις εκεινην των νασων, ενθα.

[10] κεκλημαι for ειμι, not an unusual signification. Hippol. 2, θεα κεκλημαι Κυπρις.

[11] When she perceived it, εφρασθη, συνηκεν, εγνω, ενοησεν. Hesych.

[12] The Gods beneath he despised, by casting him out without a tomb; the Gods above, as the guardians of the rites of hospitality.

[13] Whatever was due, either on the score of friendship, or as an equivalent for his care and protection.

[14] Musgrave proposes to read προμισθιαν for προμηθιαν: the version above is in accordance with the scholiast and the paraphrast.

[15] See note on Medea 338.

[16] The story of the daughters of Danaus is well known.

[17] Of this there are two accounts given in the Scholia. The one is, that the women of Lemnos being punished by Venus with an ill savor, and therefore neglected by their husbands, conspired against them and slew them. The other is found in Herodotus, Erato, chap. 138. see also Æsch. Choephoræ, line 627, ed. Schutz.

[18] Polymestor was guilty of two crimes, αδικιας and ασεβειας, for he had both violated the laws of men, and profaned the deity of Jupiter Hospitalis. Whence Agamemnon, v. 840, hints that he is to suffer on both accounts.

και βουλομαι θεων θ' 'ουνεκ ανοσιον ξενον,
και του δικαιον, τηνδε σοι δουναι δικην.

The Chorus therefore says, Ubi contingit eundem et Justitiæ et Diis esse addictum, exitiale semper malum esse; or, as the learned Hemsterheuyse has more fully and more elegantly expressed, it, Ubi, id est, in quo, vel in quem cadit et concurrit, ut ob crimen commissum simul et humanæ justitiæ et Deorum vindictæ sit obnoxius, ac velut oppignoratus; illi certissimum exitium imminet. This sense the words give, if for ου, we read 'ου, i.e. in the sense of 'οπου. MUSGRAVE. Correct Dindorf's text to 'ου.

[19] συμπεσεειν in unum coire, coincidere. In this sense it is used also, Herod. Euterpe, chap. 49.

[20] The verbal adjective in τος is almost universally used in a passive sense; ‘υποπτος, however, in this place is an exception to the rule, as are also, καλυπτης, Soph. Antig. 1011, μεμπτος, Trachin. 446.

[21] Perhaps the preferable way is to make κακοισιν agree with ανθρωποις understood; that the sense may be, You are a bad man to talk of your advantage as a plea for having acted thus.

[22] Θανουσα δ' η ζωσ' ενθαδ' εκπλησω βιον; a similar expression occurs in the Anthologia.

σιγων παρερχου τον ταλαιπωρον βιον,
αυτος σιωπηι τον χρονον μιμουμενος,
λαθων δε και βιωσον. ει δε μη, θανων.

[23] The place of her burial was called Cynosema, a promontory of the Thracian Chersonese. It was here that the Athenians gained a naval victory over the Peloponnesians and Syracusans, in the twenty-first year of the Peloponnesian war. Thucydides, book viii.

Euripides – A Short Biography

Euripides is rightly lauded as one of the great dramatists of all time. In his lifetime, he wrote over 90 plays and although only 18 have survived they reveal the scope and reach of his genius.

Euripides is identified with many theatrical innovations that have influenced drama all the way down to modern times, especially in the representation of traditional, mythical heroes as ordinary people in extraordinary circumstances. This new approach led him to pioneer developments that later writers would adapt to comedy. Yet he also became "the most tragic·of poets", focusing on the inner lives and motives of his characters in a way previously unknown. He was "the creator of...that cage which is the theatre of Shakespeare's Othello, Racine's Phèdre, of Ibsen and Strindberg," in which "...imprisoned men and women destroy each other by the intensity of their loves and hates", and yet he was also the literary ancestor of comic dramatists as diverse as Menander and George Bernard Shaw.

As would be expected from a life lived 2,500 years ago, details of it are few and far between. Accounts of his life, written down the ages, do exist but whether much is reliable or surmised is open to debate.

Most accounts agree that he was born on Salamis Island around 480 BC, to mother Cleito and father Mnesarchus, a retailer who lived in a village near Athens. Upon the receipt of an oracle saying that his son was fated to win "crowns of victory", Mnesarchus insisted that the boy should train for a career in athletics.

His education was not only confined to athletics: he also studied painting and philosophy under the masters Prodicus and Anaxagoras.

However, what became quickly very clear was that athletics was not to be his way to win crowns of victory. Euripides had been lucky enough to have been born in the era as the other two masters of Greek Tragedy; Sophocles and Æschylus. It was in their footsteps that he was destined to follow.

His first play was performed some thirteen years after the first of Socrates plays and a mere three years after Æschylus had written his classic The Oristria.

Theatre was becoming a very important part of the Greek culture. The Dionysia, held annually, was the most important festival of theatre and second only to the fore-runner of the Olympic games, the Panathenia, held every four years, in its appeal. It was a large festival in ancient Athens in honor of the god Dionysus, the central events of which were the theatrical performances of dramatic tragedies and, from 487 BC, comedies. The Dionysia actually consisted of two related festivals, the Rural Dionysia and the City Dionysia, which took place in different parts of the year.

Euripides first competed in the City Dionysia, in 455 BC, one year after the death of Æschylus, and, incredibly, it was not until 441 BC that he won first prize. His final competition in Athens was in 408 BC. However, The Bacchae and Iphigenia in Aulis were performed after his death in 405 BC and first prize was awarded posthumously. Altogether his plays won first prize only five times.

His plays, and those of Æschylus and Sophocles, indicate a difference in outlook between the three men, most easily explained as a generational gap, although with three great talents overlapping the driving forces may have pushed individual styles onwards perhaps faster than they may otherwise have done. Æschylus still looked back to the archaic period, Sophocles was in transition between periods, and Euripides was fully bonded with the new spirit of the classical age. When Euripides' plays are sequenced in time, they also show a developing pattern:

An early period of high tragedy (Medea, Hippolytus)
A patriotic period at the outset of the Peloponnesian War (Children of Hercules, Suppliants)
A middle period of disillusionment at the senselessness of war (Hecuba, Women of Troy)
An escapist period with a focus on romantic intrigue (Ion, Iphigenia in Tauris, Helen)
A final period of tragic despair (Orestes, Phoenician Women, Bacchae)

However, with over three quarters of his plays lost it is difficult to be certain as to whether the other works would also represent this development (e.g., Iphigenia at Aulis is dated with the 'despairing' Bacchae, yet it contains elements that became typical of New Comedy). In the Bacchae, he restores the chorus and messenger speech to their traditional role in the tragic plot, and the play appears to be the culmination of a regressive or archaizing tendency in his later works.

In one of his earliest surviving plays, Medea, includes a speech that he seems to have written in defence of himself as an intellectual ahead of his time, and to further challenge the times he has put the words in the mouth of the play's heroine:

"If you introduce new, intelligent ideas to fools, you will be thought frivolous, not intelligent. On the other hand, if you do get a reputation for surpassing those who are supposed to be intellectually sophisticated, you will seem to be a thorn in the city's flesh. This is what has happened to me."— Medea.

As we know Athenian tragedies during Euripides' lifetime were a public contest between playwrights. The state funded that contest and awarded prizes to the winners. The language was spoken and sung verse, the performance area included a circular floor or orchestra where the chorus could dance, a space for actors (usually three speaking actors in Euripides' time), a backdrop or skene and some special effects: an ekkyklema (used to bring the skene's "indoors" outdoors) and a mechane (used to lift actors in the air, as in deus ex machina). With the introduction of the third actor (an innovation attributed to Sophocles), acting also began to be regarded as a skill to be rewarded with prizes, requiring a long apprenticeship in the chorus. Euripides and other playwrights accordingly composed more and more arias for accomplished actors to sing and this tendency becomes more marked in his later plays: tragedy for him was a living and ever-changing genre.

Accounts by the famed comic poet, Aristophanes, characterise Euripides as a spokesman for destructive, new ideas, that mirror or help to bring about declining standards in both society and tragedy. However, 5th century tragedy was a social gathering for "carrying out quite publicly the maintenance and development of mental infrastructure" and it offered spectators a "platform for an utterly unique form of institutionalized discussion". A dramatist's role was not just to entertain but also to educate his fellow citizens—he was expected to have a message. Clearly this use of drama to democratize discussion was a very useful tool for all sides. Traditional myth provided the subject matter but the dramatist was meant to be innovative so as to sustain interest, which led to novel characterization of heroic figures and to use the mythical past to talk about present issues. The difference between Euripides and his older colleagues was, again, one of degree: his characters talked about the present more controversially and more pointedly than did those of Æschylus and Sophocles, sometimes even challenging the democratic order. Thus, for example, Odysseus is represented in Hecuba as "agile-minded, sweet-talking, demos-pleasing" i.e., a type of the war-time demagogues that were active in Athens during the Peloponnesian War. His concept is pleasingly simple. He retains the old stories and myths as well as the great names of the past and places them in the lives of contemporary Athenians thereby immediately help the audience understand it from the point of view of their own lives.

As mouthpieces for contemporary issues, they all seem to have had at least an elementary course in public speaking. Sometimes the dialogue often contrasts so strongly with the mythical and heroic setting, it looks as if Euripides aimed at parody, as for example in The Trojan Women, where the heroine's rationalized prayer provokes comment from Menelaus:

Hecuba:....O Zeus, whether you are the Law of Necessity in nature, or the Law of Reason in man, hear my prayers. You are everywhere, pursuing your noiseless path, ordering the affairs of mortals according to justice.

Menelaus: What's this? You are starting a new fashion in prayer.

Athenian citizens were familiar with rhetoric in the assembly and law courts, and some scholars believe that Euripides was more interested in his characters as speakers with cases to argue than as characters with lifelike personalities. They are self-conscious about speaking formally and their rhetoric is shown to be flawed, as if Euripides was exploring the problematical nature of language and communication: "For speech points in three different directions at once, to the speaker, to the person addressed, to the features in the world it describes, and each of these directions can be felt as skewed". Thus in the example above, Hecuba presents herself as a sophisticated intellectual describing a rationalised cosmos yet the speech is ill-matched to her audience, Menelaus (an unsophisticated listener), and soon it is found not to suit the cosmos either (her infant grandson is brutally murdered by the victorious Greeks).

Æschylus and Sophocles were innovative, but Euripides could move easily between tragic, comic, romantic and political effects, a versatility that appears in individual plays and also over the course of his career. Potential for comedy lay in his use of 'contemporary' characters, in his sophisticated tone, his relatively informal Greek, and his ingenious use of plots centered on motifs that later became standard, such as the 'recognition scene'. Other tragedians also used recognition scenes but they were heroic in emphasis, as in Æschylus's The Libation Bearers, which Euripides parodied with his mundane treatment of it in Electra (Euripides was unique among the tragedians in incorporating theatrical criticism in his plays). Traditional myth, with its exotic settings, heroic adventures and epic battles, offered potential for romantic melodrama as well as for political comments on a war theme, so that his plays are an extraordinary mix of elements. The Trojan Women for example is a powerfully disturbing play on the theme of war's horrors, apparently critical of Athenian imperialism (it was composed in the aftermath of the Melian massacre and during the preparations for the Sicilian Expedition) yet it features the comic exchange between Menelaus and Hecuba quoted above and the chorus considers Athens, the "blessed land of Theus", to be a desirable refuge—such complexity and ambiguity are typical both of his "patriotic" and "anti-war" plays.

Tragic poets in the 5th century competed against one another at the City Dionysia, each with a tetralogy consisting of three tragedies and a satyr-play. The few extant fragments of satyr-plays attributed to Æschylus and Sophocles indicate that these were a loosely structured, simple and jovial form of entertainment. However, in Cyclops (the only complete Euripides satyr-play that survives) the entertainment is structured more like a tragedy and introduced a note of critical irony typical of his other work. His genre-bending inventiveness is shown above all in Alcestis, a blend of tragic and satyric elements. This fourth play in his tetralogy for 438 BC (i.e., it occupied the position conventionally reserved for satyr-plays) is a "tragedy" that features Heracles as a satyric hero in conventional satyr-play scenes, involving an arrival, a banquet, a victory over an ogre (in this case, Death), a happy ending, a feast and a departure to new adventures.

Euripides was also a great lyric poet. In Medea, for example, he composed for his city, Athens, "the noblest of her songs of praise". His lyric skills however are not just confined to individual poems: "A play of Euripides is a musical whole....one song echoes motifs from the preceding song, while introducing new ones."

Much of his life and his whole career coincided with the struggle between Athens and Sparta for hegemony in Greece but he didn't live to see the final defeat of his city.

It is said that he died in Macedonia after being attacked by the Molossian hounds of King Archelaus and that his cenotaph near Piraeus was struck by lightning—signs of his unique powers, whether for good or ill. In an account by Plutarch, the complete failure of the Sicilian expedition led Athenians to trade renditions of Euripides' lyrics to their enemies in return for food and drink (Life of Nicias 29). Plutarch is the source also for the story that the victorious Spartan generals, having planned the demolition of Athens and the enslavement of its people, grew merciful after being entertained at a banquet by lyrics from Euripides' play Electra: "they felt that it would be a barbarous act to annihilate a city which produced such men" (Life of Lysander).

In The Frogs, composed after Euripides and Æschylus were both dead, Aristophanes imagines the god Dionysus venturing down to Hades in search of a good poet to bring back to Athens. After a debate between the two deceased bards, the god brings Æschylus back to life as more useful to Athens on account of his wisdom, rejecting Euripides as merely clever. Such comic 'evidence' suggests that Athenians admired Euripides even while they mistrusted his intellectualism, at least during the long war with Sparta.

Euripides had a famous library—one of the first to be privately collected. Although he lived most of his life in the midst of the cultured society of Athens, and was in some respects a leader in it, he grew bitter and despondent over the fierce rivalries and greedy ambitions which ran through the city. He loved the seclusion of his house at Salamis, where it was said that he composed his dramas in a cave.

Euripides fell out of favour with his fellow Athenian citizens and retired to the court of Archelaus, king of Macedon, who treated him with consideration and affection.

At his death, in around 406BC, he was mourned by the king, who, refusing the request of the Athenians that his remains be carried back to the Greek city, buried him with much splendor within his own dominions. His tomb was placed at the confluence of two streams, near Arethusa in Macedonia, and a cenotaph was built to his memory on the road from Athens towards the Piraeus.

Euripides – A Concise Bibliography

Alcestis (438 BC)
Medea (431 BC)
Heracleidae (c. 430 BC)
Hippolytus (428 BC)
Andromache (c. 425 BC)
Hecuba (c. 424 BC)
The Suppliants (c. 423 BC)
Electra (c. 420 BC)
Heracles (c. 416 BC)
The Trojan Women (c. 415 BC)
Iphigenia in Tauris (c. 414 BC)
Ion (c. 414 BC)
Helen (c. 412 BC)
Phoenician Women (c. 410 BC)
Orestes (c.408 BC)
Bacchae (405 BC)
Iphigenia at Aulis (405 BC)
Rhesus
Cyclops

Lost and Fragmentary Plays (Dated)

Peliades (455 BC)
Telephus (438 BC with Alcestis)
Alcmaeon in Psophis (438 BC with Alcestis)
Cretan Women (438 with Alcestis)
Cretans (c. 435 BC)
Philoctetes (431 BC with Medea)
Dictys (431 BC with Medea)
Theristai (satyr play, 431 BC with Medea)
Stheneboea (before 429 BC)
Bellerophon (c. 430 BC)
Cresphontes (ca. 425 BC)
Erechtheus (422 BC)
Phaethon (c. 420 BC)
Wise Melanippe (c. 420 BC)
Alexandros (415 BC with Trojan Women)
Palamedes (415 BC with Trojan Women)
Sisyphus (satyr play, 415 BC with Trojan Women)
Captive Melanippe (c. 412 BC)

Andromeda (412 BC with Helen)
Antiope (c. 410 BC)
Archelaus (c. 410 BC)
Hypsipyle (c. 410 BC)
Alcmaeon in Corinth (c. 405 BC) Won first prize as part of a trilogy with The Bacchae and Iphigenia in Aulis.

Lost and Fragmentary Plays (Not Dated)

Aegeus
Aeolus
Alcmene
Alope, or Cercyon
Antigone
Auge
Autolycus
Busiris
Cadmus
Chrysippus
Danae
Epeius
Eurystheus
Hippolytus Veiled
Ino
Ixion
Lamia
Licymnius
Meleager
Mysians
Oedipus
Oeneus
Oenomaus
Peirithous
Peleus
Phoenix
Phrixus
Pleisthenes
Polyidus
Protesilaus
Reapers
Rhadamanthys
Sciron
Scyrians
Syleus
Temenidae
Temenos
Tennes
Theseus
Thyestes

www.ingramcontent.com/pod-product-compliance
Lightning Source LLC
Chambersburg PA
CBHW060102050426
42448CB00011B/2586